Nth Home

GW00503611

Kaye Lau

BookLeaf
Publishing

Presentation by *BookLeaf Publishing*

Web: www.bookleafpub.com

E-mail: info@bookleafpub.com

ISBN: 9789357617543

First edition 2022

To every expat in Shanghai

ACKNOWLEDGEMENT

Special thanks to Jeffery Leung for illustrating the book cover, and to Sam Riddle for reading my creative writing journal entries in 12th grade.

PREFACE

Nth Home explores the themes of change (or lack thereof), situational loneliness, dwelling in the past, and the meaning of home, through various forms of poetry.

Can't, Oh

In my new home, I've planted a seed;
Like the old ones that fell in places,
Those of which that nobody will read.

My mark is a house and family.
I have been fed and taught all I know,
But those I carry so heavily.

After each year, I'm given away.
A new spawn point, and a new checkpoint
That evoke joy for less than a day.

I make myself so comfortable,
Gain new friends, and learn a new culture,
But none of these things are portable.

Columns and rows of off-white dwellings,
Which I know of, but will never fill
What I hear of each person's tellings.

In front of me is another place,
Another move, new set of parents,
And I will have forgotten my base.

I cannot walk from house to old house,
But today on this cool, daily stroll,
A detail holds my eye; a girl's blouse.

I pull over to where she's standing,
And call out as loud as I can, till
I realize my sounds aren't landing.

Because although that was once my time,
It happened and won't happen again.
I lost my home, long before my prime.

So, I slowly trudge back to that room,
Which I have reluctantly called home.
It's nice but feels like impending doom.

On the way, I see a dog in cone.
She's old, but has stayed one family.
Her life is what I would like to own.

My experiences are so vast;
I meet and know so many people,
But all ends, and it's over so fast.

But Unfortunately

if only I let it last just a few more seconds

who knows how long more

if only it weren't for me, then maybe just maybe

my tears would drip not pour

but unfortunately I can't glue the photos down

I'm so helpless and I let the smile turn into a
frown

I am physically in so much pain because of my
emotions

and it doesn't help the distance is between a
couple oceans

if only I got three more months at the top of
twenty two

I could have seen you more

I wish I could slow down time to keep me here
forever

give these years an encore

but unfortunately I have to give up my denial

take my change, push on forward, stop blocking
the aisle

I am not ready at all despite this ride I'm
embarking

and I promise again that my eyes aren't
sparkling

I'm laughing, I'm smiling

but I can't help turning misty

oh, what a joy it is to laugh underwater

on the other side of the equator

my eyes are bloodshot from crying all night

I'm sure the cat outside could hear me

it scares me that there's not a next time planned

do not tell me that you disagree

I am folding it in to try and cut myself out
smoothly

and it doesn't help that I can barely tell my story
loosely

October 3

Six twenty one memorabilia
Amanda to Becca to Celia
Fitted characters or my archetype
Struggling inside my thin and shallow pipe

(Star)gazing

Clouds abundant daily

Heartbeats skipping gaily

One hundred and first draft

I thought I saw a shooting star, but it was an
aircraft

Throwing my head back, I took a deep, hefty
breath, and laughed

Spotting not a cardinal, but just a cardinal smear

I thought there was something in my eye, but it
was a tear

Vision almost unclear

Tangled strands unruly

Muddled thoughts unduly

Don't See Me

Don't see me
Pass you by
So merry
I don't buy
No one's free
Or they lie

Sunset tea
Sunrise sigh
Morning glee
Midnight cry
Don't see me
Say goodbye

Again?

So many options, so few opportune.

Can I do more than just singing in tune?

So what, if I can? Does it really matter?

I hear too many voices, too much chatter.

Still on the find, continuing the grind.

I came in blind, but will I go out blind?

What do I want, and where do I want to go?

Might as well try, the stakes aren't high for "no."

Fake Scenarios of the Past

I'm thinking of a spice that's not spicy.
Numbs not my tongue nor lips, but all my fears.
Bright family shop, where nothing's pricey.
Joy and delight, but I wish they were tears.

I'm thinking of the sounds of tomorrow,
Following the future, flying with mist.
Now they are yesterday, so long ago;
So, did my memories even exist?

I'm thinking of the few sights in the sky;
Layers of pale hide away the morning.
Zero stars, but a thousand planes fly by,
Looming over like a global warning.

It's the past, and it's fake, you might ask how,
But they are fake because they are not now.

I feel lonely

standing while waiting
watching the leaves fly
glaring at the sun
holding in a sigh
wanting something, but not knowing what

today's meeting point
three-thirty pm
woke up this morning
eleven am
people around, but I feel lonely

each and every one
I'm so happy for
say hi while passing
I can't ask for more
needing something, but living without

waves of salty sweet
floods of bitter feels
coming back right here
everyday new meals
what is lonely, if not knowing home?

Roomful of Actors

Dear Observation Journal,

I saw everyone, but no one saw me.
In my corner, I sat still,
I noticed; I wondered if they did too.

I think I constantly search
During each minute and every second.
I am looking for something,
But I pretend not to realize it.

Sometimes, I leave, go outside,
And I notice a familiar face.
And that's it, there's no "and then."

Sincerely, doing an assignment, Me

it is not ours

let's not keep in touch
once we leave, we leave
i do not miss much
neither will i grieve

overreaction
toxicity, fun
i'll try subtraction
minus them, leave one

that one is just me
i have no more time
why can't you guys see
without this i'll climb

and so this cycle
repeats like hist'ry
heavy icicle
melts into myst'ry

Childhood Friends

all my childhood friends
have grown up
and relationships come to ends

they're popular, they're adult, they're "cool"
almost like they've abandoned me
and here I am, a fool
still the same, still awkward, still a baby

they've accomplished
I'm demolished
they've changed
I'm still strange

they're excelling, they're winners, they're off
almost stars in the sky, I see
and I'm left in the rough
still behind, still struggling, still me

but at least I still know
what it's like to be a child
I will decide when it's my time to grow

Spoon in the Road

After walking for eighteen hours, she
encountered a fork in the road.

Unlike the side character, it did not take her very
long to decide.

Yes, she's the main character, and the path is
written for her.

All she needed to do was to close her eyes, and
enjoy the ride.

On to the left she went, not regretting picking it
over the right.

The only thing she mourned over was the
straight path behind.

If the single path was just a little longer, would
this story be better?

Regardless, she walked quickly, excited for what
she would find.

Each new sight created a new memory on the
road to the left.

Moment upon moment upon eighteen thousand
trees and flowers.

She continued at a brisk pace with minimal stops
for breaks,

Happily feeling every wind and soaking in all
the rain showers.

After a while, she found there were three new
paths in front of her.

Without hesitation, she headed down the left
path with a hum.

After a while, she thought of the side character
whom she'd left,

but she could not dwell on sad things; that was
her rule of thumb.

Minutes to hours to ambulatory moment in the sun on the grass.

She greeted the same flowers and said hello to the same trees.

Deja vu turned from dream to nightmare when she turned the corner,

Walking on the hard road, no longer with the feeling of ease.

She thought to herself, "why has my destination not appeared yet?

I've gone through thick and thin, mastered every fall and every climb."

It was then she realized it was not a fork in the road from yesterday.

Because she's been walking in a circle of a spoon the entire time.

Shower Thoughts

If I sang too loud,
Would the people next door hear?
What about crying?

Period Thoughts

Oh, hello, again.
Is this calling attention
To quiet drama?

About Ghosts

empty seats hold nobody's ghost.
the leaves outside chatter like children,
while I sit and think, unlike most.

the wind blows the leaves in the cold;
every child wails like a ghost undead,
feeling a rough smoothness unfold.

a chair in the corner pulled out;
not a soul stands up and runs away
to wonder what it's all about.

Gray Skies

I'm missing gray skies
the third day of green
no sun in my eyes
it's all on the screen

polluted purple
fall on and make us
run in a circle
but I want that fuss

being stuck all year
perhaps worse than this
fear of feeling fear
which I kind of miss

Groundhog Day

Groundhog day
Nowhere to stay
It's the same all day
Everyday

Everyday's the same
What day is today?
I play all the same games
Then go back and lay
On my bed for the day
It's time for lunch again
Meal to meal and then
I'm living life on the edge
Of my mini balcony ledge

Groundhog day
Is it April or May?
I slept the day
Away

Everyday's the same
What day is today?
I play all the same games
Then go back and lay
On my bed for the day
It's time for lunch again
Meal to meal and then
I'm living life on the edge
Of my mini balcony ledge

It feels like it's February second
And tomorrow's still the same, I reckon
Over and over again
Groceries that just won't send
Eyes open in my bed
And I don't know if I can

It feels like it's February second
And tomorrow's still the same, I reckon
Over and over again
When will this awful year end
Counting days by the second
But I know that I can

Groundhog day
Everyday restarts
But I have all this time
To come up with a rhyme,
Put on a one-person show
I really don't know
What I'm doing though
But it's fine 'cause it's
(Groundhog day)

the white sky

the white sky, the sun's throne
a soft serve ice cream cone
waiting, standing alone

slightly windy, light rain
a pack of processed grain
trying to ignore pain

Disneytown

Magic loops of music
So many emotions
They make time go too quick
With light-hearted reactions

Turning frowns upside-down
Cooling off all the heat
The subject's Disneytown
But it's more bitter than sweet

Fallen Petals

petals taped back on
they're tight, but they're still falling
and then they are gone

change

people change
feelings change
it is strange
this odd range

but like the day
always setting
it is okay
I'm not fretting